Child Labor
in America

Edited by Juliet H. Mofford

A young sweeper and a doffer, by Lewis Hine
(Courtesy of the Library of Congress)

Discovery Enterprises, Ltd.
Carlisle, Massachusetts

© Discovery Enterprises, Ltd., Carlisle, MA 1997

ISBN 1-878668-98-6 paperback edition
Library of Congress Catalog Card Number 97-67313

10   9   8   7   6   5   4   3   2   1

Printed in the United States of America

Subject Reference Guide:

Child Labor in America
edited by Juliet H. Mofford

Child Labor — U. S. History

Street Children — U. S. History

Lewis Wickes Hine — Social Photographer

Jacob Riis — U. S. History

Mother Jones — U. S. History

Child Stars — U. S. History

Photo Credits:

Cover photo: New York City news boys, by Lewis Hine
(Library of Congress)

Photos are credited where they appear in the text.

Table of Contents

Think of the deadly drudgery. Children rise at half-past four, commanded by the ogre scream of the factory whistle; they hurry, ill fed, unkempt, unwashed, half dressed to the walls which shut out the day and which confine them amid the din and dust and merciless maze of the machines.

— Julia E. Johnsen,
Selected Articles on Child Labor
(New York: H. W. Wilson, 1925), p. 79.

Preparing beans for canning, by Lewis Hine, 1910.
(Library of Congress)

Declaration of Dependence By the Children of America in Mines and Factories and Workshops

Whereas, We, Children of America, are declared to have been born free and equal, and

Whereas, We are yet in bondage in this land of the free; are forced to toil the long day or the long night, with no control over the conditions of labor, as to health or safety or hours or wages, and with no right to the rewards of our service, therefore be it

Resolved I - That childhood is endowed with certain inherent and inalienable rights, among which are freedom from toil for daily bread; the right to play and to dream; the right to the normal sleep of the night season; the right to an education, that we may have equality of opportunity for developing all that there is in us of mind and heart.

Resolved II - That we declare ourselves to be helpless and dependent; that we are and of right ought to be dependent, and that we hereby present the appeal of our helplessness that we may be protected in the enjoyment of the rights of childhood.

Resolved III - That we demand the restoration of our rights by the abolition of child labor in America.

— National Child Labor Committee, 1913

Foreword

The golf links lie so near the mill
That nearly every day
The laboring children can look out
And see the men at play.

— Sarah N. Cleghorn

Children have always worked in America. Colonial children worked alongside parents to help produce the family's food and clothing. The success of frontier settlements required all hands. Today, most young people do their share by cleaning their rooms, setting the table, sorting laundry, shoveling snow, cleaning the garage, or doing yard work. Such chores are not what is meant by child labor in this book. Modern teenagers earn spending money by working at fast food restaurants or baby sitting, yet seldom become victims of the abuses suffered by millions of youngsters in the past.

Although child labor existed before the Civil War, it expanded dramatically from 1870 through World War I, as the United States developed into a world industrial power. Work itself had moved from family farms into factories and, as manufacturing increased, so did the demand for more workers to run the machines and mine the coal. Before long, children as young as ten were working twelve or more hours, six days-a-week. Some factories even had whipping rooms for little workers who became lazy. Children caught talking or giggling saw their wages cut. During the long days and nights, cold water splashed in children's faces woke them up and got them back on the job.

Traditional attitudes passed down from previous generations also contributed to the rise of the child labor in America. Adults generally viewed work as excellent moral training for youngsters. Work would teach children responsibility and keep them out of mischief. Did not their religious principles preach that idle hands were the devil's playthings? This Puritan work ethic remains a theme common to American culture. Many in the 19th century considered child labor a national asset, necessary for forging the country's financial prosperity.

Soon, it became easier for children than for their fathers to find jobs, since children could be hired for less. Children took jobs away from men who needed higher wages to support families. Child labor kept everyone's wages down and created a cycle of poverty in which families depended on their childrens' paychecks to survive. Employers got more work done for less money, thus increasing their profits in a competitive market.

The U. S. Census of 1870 reported that 750,000 children, ages ten to fifteen, were employed by industry. Even more children were at work in fields, where, sun-up to sundown, they performed stoop-labor (picking crops). This statistic did not even include children under ten, nor youngsters working in sweat-shops, or as street vendors. These little laborers were simply "off the books."

By 1880, 1,118,000 children under sixteen, or one out of every six, comprised part of the American labor force.

Mills and mines were dirty and dangerous. Even though employers insisted small bodies and nimble fingers could do these jobs best, children in the workplace suffered three times as many accidents as adults. Small hands were easily crushed by speeding machines that lacked safety devices. Frail bodies became sleepy and slid underneath moving machinery and equipment. Employers were seldom held responsible by safety rules and rarely concerned themselves with the health and safety of their work force. Anyone injured on the job could be easily replaced by another from the increasing numbers of immigrants who arrived daily on American shores.

Some jobs, more hazardous than others, were known as the "Dangerous Trades." In canneries, children worked alongside parents, peeling tomatoes and snipping beans with sharp knives or capping forty cans a minute as they passed by on assembly lines. Shucking oysters or picking and peeling icy shrimp scratched and cut small hands. Children as young as four regularly worked in tobacco factories.

Glass factories were known as "Glory Holes," because heat from open furnaces reached 130 degrees Fahrenheit. Owners insisted they had to run these factories around the clock in order to make any profit, so young boys employed in such work frequently slept on factory floors.

After watching glass workers, Florence Kelley said, "The picture of these little figures moving about in the shadows, carrying trays of glass, cutting

A young, glass factory worker, Alexandria, VA, by Lewis Hine
(Library of Congress)

themselves occasionally upon broken glass in the dark, or being burned by the hot bottles, are images that influenced my life's work as a crusader against child labor."

By 1842, Connecticut had limited children's working hours to ten a day. Other states passed laws, but regulations were seldom enforced and employers who hired children under the legal age limit were rarely fined. Laws were continually broken, not only by managers of mills and mines, but by parents themselves. Working class and immigrant families typically counted on their children to help support the family. Although state mandates required employees to be fourteen or sixteen years of age, parents got work permits forged and advised their children to exaggerate ages. Managers hired men to forge "proof papers," phony documents with later birth dates, which families purchased because they depended on children's wages to contribute toward food and rent. Parents frequently took their smaller children into factories to work as "assistants." It will never be known how many thousands of children worked off the books, receiving no compensation except a few extra dollars in their mothers' pay envelopes.

Educational reformers campaigned for laws that would require children to remain in school. Connecticut passed a law requiring basic instruction for factory children as early as 1813. Massachusetts decreed in 1836 that, "No child under the age of fifteen years shall be employed in any manufacturing establishment...unless such child shall have attended public or private day school...at least 3 months out of 12 months." By 1850, Rhode Island and Pennsylvania had similar laws.

The first compulsory school attendance law was passed in Massachusetts in 1852. However, it was one thing for a state to provide free public education and quite another matter to get children into the schools. The greatest obstacle to education was the prevalence of child labor. Arguments arose over the constitutional right of states to compel children to attend school when parents preferred them to be working. Some businesses relocated South, where labor was cheaper and managers could escape New England's stricter education laws.

Other employers attempted to satisfy educational reforms by setting up night schools in their factories — but students frequently fell asleep at their desks. After a long day of work, the children had little ability to concentrate, little energy left for learning. Factory representatives were often sent into schools to coax children to drop out and enter mills, for when it came to prioritizing a child's education or another pay envelope for the family, mill or mine was usually chosen over classroom.

By 1881, only seven states had passed laws requiring children to be at least twelve before they went out to work for wages. Yet the only proof of age required was a statement from parents. The Society for the Prevention of Cruelty to Children drafted a factory bill for the New York State Legislature in 1884 that would limit the hours of all employees under twenty-one to a ten-hour workday and a sixty-hour week. All younger than fourteen were to be kept out of the factories. This proposal died because many businesses insisted that New York companies would no longer be able to compete against states employing child workers and would move their factories out-of-state.

In 1886, New York passed the Factory Act, which prohibited children under thirteen from factory work and required children to produce affidavits proving their ages. However, this only applied to factories in rural areas and the two factory inspectors appointed to enforce it could not possibly cover the whole state. To avoid problems, employers customarily trained their child workers to hide whenever the factory inspector appeared.

By 1900, American industry was supported by 1,752,187 child laborers. There was a growing national awareness of the need to draft child labor laws. The Reverend Edgar G. Murphy (1869-1913), an Episcopal minister from Montgomery, Alabama, founded the Alabama Child Labor Committee and became a chief organizer of the National Child Labor Committee. Due to Murphy's influence, Alabama, North and South Carolina, and Georgia passed child labor laws in 1901. Although these laws were backed by labor unions, they failed to take hold because state legislatures did not want government telling them how to run their businesses. Murphy and his fellow reformers persisted and by 1903, five southern states had passed laws establishing fourteen as the minimum age for children to work in factories. Yet children of ten who were orphans or could prove their work "necessary to the family," were exempt. Without compulsory education laws, the children could not be required to remain in school.

Reformers like Murphy, nicknamed "Child-savers" by the press, continued to push states to pass laws restricting child labor. Eventually, they realized that only the federal government could provide truly effective and permanent legislation to protect children. The National Child Labor Committee (NCLC) was formed in 1904 and chartered by Congress in 1907. Federal child labor laws were drafted as early as 1904, but it proved a long, tough battle to get any legislation passed that would become law in all states. Some Congressmen argued that any laws banning child labor meant that boys and girls would refuse to help with any household chores.

Child-savers believed that allowing children to work in factories and mines or as street vendors and in shops, was "immoral." Reformers claimed "the profits of American industry are based upon the enslavement of children." As they saw it, working children were being deprived of opportunities which were the rights of all Americans. Child-savers insisted all children had "the right to childhood," and that youngsters who worked instead of attending school were "doomed to a life of poverty," because they would never learn the skills necessary to improve their economic condition. In the opinion of these social reformers, the health of child laborers, indeed, their very lives, were at risk.

The NCLC's first task was to educate the public, which seemed to be unaware of child labor abuses. Child-savers thought that once Americans understood the situation, they would demand reform. The NCLC set about to investigate conditions throughout the nation, focusing first on industries holding the most dangers for child employees: coal mines, glass factories, canneries, textile mills, night time telegram delivery, street trades, and farm labor.

In 1910, the NCLC developed the Uniform Child Labor Law, which combined the best of the protective laws of Massachusetts, New York, and Illinois. This set the minimum age at fourteen for manufacturing jobs and ten in mining. Work was to be limited to eight hours for fourteen through sixteen year-olds. Night work was to be prohibited for anyone under the age of sixteen. Documentary proof of age was to be required, rather than simply relying on parents' words. Yet, that same year, the census showed that two million children between ten and fifteen were employed in factories, farms, and mines.

Between 1911 and 1913, thirty-nine states passed some laws restricting child labor, but the laws contained loopholes. For example, most included a poverty provision allowing exemption. This said that children under fourteen would be permitted to work if their families depended upon their wages. Another way to get around laws stipulating that no child could be required to work more than ten hours a day was for bosses to simply tell authorities that the child's overtime hours were "voluntary." Younger children could legally work with their parent's consent, or if they were orphans.

The NCLC sought to establish a federal children's bureau to collect information on topics related to child welfare and the rights of children. The bill to set up this national agency gained public support following President Theodore Roosevelt's endorsement and the first White House Conference on the Care of Dependent Children in 1909. Yet, it failed to receive support from the Society for the Prevention of Cruelty to Children, as well as most manufacturers, because it seemed to give federal government too much power over individual states.

Congress passed the bill to create the Children's Bureau, which was signed into law by President Taft in April of 1912, after some children who had participated in the Lawrence, MA Textile Strike testified before Congress. Under the Department of Commerce and Labor, the Children's Bureau was charged to

12

"investigate and report on all matters pertaining to the welfare of children among all classes of our people, and shall especially investigate questions of infant mortality, the birth rate, orphanages, juvenile courts, desertion, dangerous occupations, accidents and diseases of children, and employment..."

The first federal laws against child labor, passed by Congress and signed by President Woodrow Wilson in 1916 and 1919, were declared unconstitutional a few years later by the United States Supreme Court. It took Franklin Delano Roosevelt's New Deal to pass the first effective laws against child labor. Under the National Industrial Recovery Act (NIRA), 1933-1935, minimum age standards were incorporated in some 500 separate industrial codes. This resulted in a dramatic decrease in the number of working children and in January of 1934, FDR announced "child labor has been abolished." Unfortunately, this was not quite the case.

Special interest groups remained determined to hire children. The Non-Partisan Committee for the Ratification of the Child Labor Amendment, for example, was opposed by the National Committee for the Protection of Child, Family, School, and Church, supported by big business interests. In 1935, the Supreme Court ruled the NIRA "unconstitutional, all its Acts null and void." The Justices believed Congress had given the President too much power. Within a year, the number of employed children in the nation increased 150%.

The Fair Labor Standards Act

As well as cutting back the work week and raising minimum wage for all employees, the Fair Labor Standards Act (FLSA), which became law in June of 1938, prohibited employment of any child under the age of fourteen, except for farm work. The FLSA also made it illegal to hire children under sixteen while school was in session. Nor would any child under sixteen be permitted to work on goods shipped across state lines or sent overseas. To work at trades considered "hazardous" by the Secretary of Labor, like mining or logging, workers had to be eighteen or older. The FLSA was bitterly contested by such organizations as the Cotton Textile Institute. The National Association of Manufacturers labeled it a "communist plot" and "Nazi scheme," and attempted to get it overthrown by the Supreme Court; but the FLSA prevailed.

FLSA left a range of jobs unregulated. Farm lobby interests managed to prevent agricultural laborers from being protected by the federal government through the FLSA. The Act also failed to protect children working in restaurants, retail stores, small businesses such as laundries, street vendors, or those who delivered newspapers and groceries. FLSA was later expanded to cover children in agriculture, when it became illegal to hire anyone under sixteen for farm work during school hours, unless they were "helping their parents." Yet a Commission studying migrant labor in 1950 reported to President Harry S. Truman that 395,000 children between the ages of ten and fifteen were at work on farms.

Great progress has been made since the nineteenth century, yet the struggle against child labor continues. Although child labor is prohibited by law in nearly every country today, it continues to exist, making children" labor's outlaws." All over the world children continue to work illegally and unnoticed. Inspectors cannot possibly catch and report all underage workers. And the authorities frequently, as they have done for generations, simply look the other way.

Indentured Servants and Apprentices

Apprenticeship, a tradition dating back to Medieval Europe, was the way most young people received training in job skills prior to the Industrial Revolution. Both sides benefited from this formal agreement. The tradesman was provided with years of free labor, while his apprentice learned skills that would enable him to earn his own living as an adult. Apprenticeship was also a way for towns to provide for their poor. Children whose parents suffered hard times, or who were orphans, were customarily "bound out." The obligations of both master and apprentice — or indentured servant — were described in a legally-binding contract, such as the following indenture paper.

Source: *Manuscript Collections*, Old York Historical Society, York, ME, 1820.

This Indenture witnesseth that...Selectmen and Overseers of the poor of the Town of York in the County of York and State of Maine, by virtue of a law of the said State in such cases made and provided, have placed and by these present do place and bind out as an apprentice a poor child name Lyman Bragdon, son of Daniel Bragdon, who is lawfully settled in this Town of York, and who has become chargeable to the said Town as a pauper-unto Merret Dummer of Alna, in the County of Lincoln and State aforesaid, yeoman to learn the Art, trade, or mystery of a Farmer. The said Lyman Bragdon after the manner of an apprentice, to dwell with and serve the said Merret Dummer from the day of the date hereof until the twelfth day of June which will be in the year of our Lord one thousand eight hundred and twenty at which time said apprentice, if he should be living, will be twenty one years of age-during all which said time or term the said apprentice his said master will and faithfully shall serve, his secrets keep and his lawful commands everywhere and at all times readily obey; he shall do no damage to his said master, nor shall he knowingly suffer any to be done by others....From his said master's service he shall not absent himself without the consent of his said master-And the said Merret Dummer on his part doth hereby promise covenant and agree to teach and instruct said apprentice, or cause him to be taught and instructed in Farming or Husbandry by the best way and means he can and also to give him Common School learning, That is, he shall teach him or cause him to be taught to read, write and Cypher as far as the Rule of Three, if said apprentice has a capacity to learn and shall well and faithfully provide for said apprentice good and sufficient meat, drink, clothing, lodging, and physic and other necessaries during said term, and at the expiration thereof shall give unto said apprentice two suits of clothes, one suitable for Lord's days and the other suitable for working days...

Not all masters were kind, nor all servants obedient. Many indentured servants and apprentices ran away and when they did, were tracked down like runaway slaves. However, bondservants had a right to petition courts to report abusive masters, something black slaves could not do. The following notices appeared in early newspapers and demonstrate some options open to apprentices, as well as indicating the runaway problem.

Kennebunkport Weekly Visitor   *October 12, 1816 Ad for Runaway*

"Report on Manufactures" —1791

Alexander Hamilton, America's first Secretary of the Treasury, believed that putting children to work in the factories would not only benefit the new nation's industrial development but would also "save them from the curse of idleness." Hamilton's ideas, set forth in his "Report On Manufactures," influenced the selection of the new work force demanded by the Industrial Revolution. Child labor was considered necessary in a New Republic developing its economy independent of Europe.

Source: Barbara Mayer Wertheimer. *We Were There: The Story of Working Women in America* (New York: Pantheon, 1977), pp. 51, 78.

It is worthy of particular remark, that, in general, women and children are rendered more useful; and the latter more early useful, by manufacturing establishments, than they would otherwise be.

In 1789, the new president, George Washington, visited a factory in Boston that produced sails for ships and noted in his diary:

"Fourteen Girls spinning with both hands (the flax being fastened to their waists). Children (girls) turn the wheels for them."

That same year, a cotton factory opened in Beverly, Massachusetts,

"employing women and children — many of whom will be otherwise useless, if not burdensome to society."

Textile Tots

The Industrial Revolution brought children into the mills, where machines and managers determined the speed of work. In 1790, Samuel Slater, remembered as the "Father of American Industry," opened a spinning mill on the Blackstone River in Pawtucket, Rhode Island and hired four boys to operate his new machines. Within a week, he had expanded his labor force to seven boys and two girls between the ages of seven and twelve, working from 5:30 a.m. to 7:30 p.m., six days-a-week, for 80 cents to $1.40. Entire families were soon being hired at Slater's Mill, and other factories, for "Family Wages," or one pay check per family. The more children a family had to bring to work, the more a mill owner got for his money. Should a family decide to take a child out of the factory to attend school, the entire family might be discharged. Slater published the following ad in a Rhode Island newspaper.

"They wish to hire a weaver, capable of taking charge of water-looms. Also a Family, of from five to eight children, capable of working in a Cotton Mill. None need apply, unless well recommended."

Hine made notes on the Vianna family of Manhattan: Josephine, 9, and Nicholas, 12, are sewing on buttons. The father is wrapping a bundle of finished garments...

"The Shadow Child"

The following song by Harriet Munroe tells of a little girl cheated of childhood and doomed to work in a textile factory.

Source: *Hull House Songs*. Chicago, 1915. Found in Jane Addams, *80 Years at Hull House*. Allen F. Davis & Mary Lynn McCree, editors. (Chicago: Quadrangle Books, 1969), p. 95.

Why do the wheels go whirring round, Mother, Mother?
Oh? Mother are they giants bound,
And will they growl forever?
Yes, fiery giants underground,
Daughter, little daughter,
Forever turn the whole around
And rumble, grumble ever.
Why do I pick the threads all day, Mother, Mother?
While sunshine children laugh and play,
And must I work forever?
Yes, Shadow Child, the livelong day,
Daughter, little daughter,
Your hands must pick the threads away
And feel the sunshine never.
And is the white thread never spun, Mother, Mother?
And is the white cloth never done,
For you and me, done never?
Oh! yes, our thread will all be spun,
Daughter, little daughter,
When we lie down out in the sun,
And work no more forever.
And work no more forever.

Determined to avoid the working conditions which had brought misery to so many factory families in British textile mills, managers at Lowell, Massachusetts, "New City on the Merrimack River," recruited single girls, mostly from New England farms, to run their looms and spinning frames. In the following selection, Lucy Larcom (1824-1893), who later became a famous poet, magazine editor, and teacher, recalls working in a Lowell mill as a child. Larcom's mother, a widow, supported her large family by becoming keeper of a corporation boarding house for mill workers.

Source: Lucy Larcom, *A New England Girlhood, Outlined from Memory*. (Williamstown, MA: Corner House Publishers, 1977), pp. 153-155. Originally published by Houghton, Mifflin Company, Boston, 1889.

I heard it said by my mother, in a distressed tone, "The children will have to leave school and go into the mill."...The mill agent did not want to take us two little girls, but consented on condition we should be sure to attend school the full number of months prescribed each year. I was then between eleven and twelve years old.

I listened to all that was said about it, very much fearing that I should not be permitted to do the coveted work, (for the feeling had already come to me, that I was the one too many in the overcrowded family nest)....So I went to my first day's work in the mill with a light heart. The novelty of it made it seem easy, and it really was not hard, just to change the bobbins on the spinning frames every three quarters of an hour or so, with half a dozen other little girls who were doing the same thing. When I came back at night, the family began to pity me for my long, tiresome day's work, but I laughed and said,

"Why, it is nothing but fun. It is just like play."

And for a little while it was only a new amusement; I liked it better than going to school and "making believe." I was learning when I was not. And there was a great deal of play mixed with it. We were not occupied more than half the time. The intervals were spent frolicking around among the spinning-frames, teasing and talking to the older girls, or entertaining ourselves with games and stories in a corner, or exploring, with the overseer's permission, the mysteries of the carding-room, the dressing-room, and the weaving room.

A young mill girl
(Merrimack Valley Textile Museum)

I never cared much for machinery. The buzzing and hissing and whizzing of pulleys and rollers and spindles and flyers around me often grew tiresome. I could not see into their complications, or feel interested in them. But in a room below us we were sometimes allowed to peer in through a sort of blind door at the great waterwheel that carried the works of the whole mill. It was so huge that we could only watch a few of its spokes at a time, and part of its dripping rim, moving with a slow, measured strength through the darkness that shut it in....

There were compensations for being shut into daily toil so early. The mill itself had its lessons for us. But it was not, and could not be, the right sort of life for a child....The little money I could earn-one dollar a week, besides the price of my board, was needed in the family, and I must return to the mill...for the next six or seven years.

...and when you do the same thing twenty times-a hundred times a day, it is *so dull*!

"Bell Ballard" Goes to Work in a Cotton Mill

In 1903, Marie Van Vorst, a social reformer from New York's upper class, put on "simple work garb," took the name "Bell Ballard," and went to work in a South Carolina cotton mill. She and her sister-in-law worked at several different occupations in order to write about the lives of working women from personal experience.

Source: Mrs. John Van Vorst and Marie Van Vorst, *The Woman Who Toils: Being the Experiences of Two Ladies as Factory Girls.* (New York: Doubleday, Page & Company, 1903); found in Barbara Mayer Wertheimer, *We Were There: The Story of the Working Woman in America.* (New York: Pantheon, 1977), pp. 338-339.

One day a boy of fourteen walked beside me, so thin that his bones threatened to pierce his vestments. He had only one arm. Cotton clings to his clothes, his shoes, nearly falling off his feet, are red with clay stains. He works from 5:45 a.m. to 6:45 p.m. and makes fifty cent a day.

"It keeps me in existence," he told me.

In the midst of the grinding and pounding of the gigantic machines, I saw children who had not yet been assigned work for the day, sleeping against bales of cotton. A child of eight with bare, filthy feet worked beside me, the tobacco snuff she chewed drooling from her mouth. Her hands and arms are no longer flesh colored, but resemble weather-roughened hide, ingrained with dirt.

Van Vorst described her landlord's child working in the same textile mill:

She is seven; so small that they have a box for her to stand upon. She is a pretty, frail, little thing, a spooler....Through the frames on the other side I can only see her fingers as they clutch at the flying spools; her head is not high enough, even with the box, to be visible. Her hands are fairy hands, fine-boned, well-made, only they are so thin and dirty, and her nails-claws....A nail can be torn from the finger, is torn from the finger frequently, by this flying spool.

Van Vorst asked one little girl her age, "and the child replied, 'ten.'" She looked no more than six...children are taught to lie their ages, both by employers and by their own parents, who count on the forty cents a day the children earn to help sustain the family....The children crouched on the floor to eat. Some would fall asleep between mouthfuls of food, and lie asleep with food in their mouths until the overseer rouses them to their tasks again. Here and there totters a little child just learning to walk; it runs and crawls the length of the mill.

The children all seemed malnourished, their stomachs distended and swollen, their bones nearly through their skin. Most returned home about 8:00 p.m., or later if the mill was working overtime. They are usually beyond speech. They fall asleep at the tables, on the stairs; they are carried to bed and there laid down as they are, unwashed, undressed; and the inanimate bundles of rags so lie until the mill summons them with its imperious cry before sunrise, while they are still in stupid sleep....

In one Alabama mill, where seventy-five children work twelve hour shifts with a half-hour for lunch, the company sponsored a night school. Fifty of the seventy-five children attended, but were so tired that many fell asleep at their books. Employers blame the greed of parents for the fact that children worked in the mill, but the mothers told me that if they refused to send their children into the mills, they would be evicted from their company-owned homes....Most parents yielded to economic need and company pressure. ...Absent workers who were ill got their pay docked or were hounded out of their sick-beds to get back to their looms.

After Marie Van Vorst returned to New York, she described her experiences to a friend who had financial interest in one Southern mill. His response:

"Dear friend Marie!" he exclaimed. "Those little children love the mill! They like to work. It is a great deal better for them to be employed than for them to run the street! I believe they are really very happy at their work."

Breaker Boys in the Coal Mines

"Shut in from everything that is pleasant..."

By 1910, more than 15,000 boys below the age of sixteen were employed in coal mines. The following section describes the lot of "breaker boys," whose job it was to pick out the pieces of slate which could not be sold for fuel. This excerpt from an 1877 issue of "The Labor Standard," describes conditions at the Hickory Colliery in Pennsylvania.

Source: Found in Milton Meltzer. *Bread and Roses: The Struggle of American Labor, 1865-1915.* (New York: New American Library/Mentor, 1967), pp. 27-28.

In a little room in this big, black shed-a room not twenty feet square-forty boys are picking their lives away. The floor of the room is an inclined plane, and a stream of coal pours constantly in. They work here, in this little black hole, all day and every day, trying to keep cool in summer, trying to keep warm in winter, picking away at the black coals, bending over till their little spines are curved, never saying a word all the livelong day.

Breaker boys at work, South Pittston, PA, by Lewis Hine
(National Archives)

These little fellows go to work in this cold dreary room at seven o'clock in the morning and work till it is too dark to see any longer. For this they get $1 to $3 a week. Not three boys in this roomful could read or write. Shut in from everything that is pleasant, with no chance to learn, with no knowledge of what is going on about them, with nothing to do but work, grinding their little lives away in this dusty room, they are no more than the wire screens that separate the great lumps of coal from the small. They had no games; when their day's work is done, they are too tired for that. They know nothing but the difference between slate and coal.

Breaker boys at lunch, by Lewis Hine
(Library of Congress)

Children Work the City Streets

The Littlest Hustlers

New York City newsboys, by Lewis Hine
(Library of Congress)

There were plenty of job opportunities for kids on city streets. Jobs like selling candy, fruit or flowers, collecting junk, and delivering groceries or telegrams would eventually be taken over by adults with shoe stands, junkman's carts, and convenience stores. Other street trades were replaced by modern vending machines and telephones, but from the 1850s through the First World War, America's city streets were filled with "little hustlers." Reformers fretted over the bad influences of street life upon these children, but most Americans admired the enterprising "little merchants." However, few attended school long enough to gain the skills for a brighter economic future. Many children who worked the city streets were homeless or orphaned. They slept in abandoned buildings and alleyways and scavenged food from saloons and grocery carts. By 1915, seventeen states and several cities had passed laws against child street-traders.

The Newsies

Exhausted newsboy sleeps on the subway steps, by Lewis Hine
(Library of Congress)

Until the 1920s, when adult newsstands became common, publishers depended on "newsies" for their distribution. Boys, and to a lesser extent, girls, peddled papers at all hours of day and night, in all kinds of weather. Some lived in special Newsboys Lodging Homes, while others slept on streets so they could pick up morning editions, hot off the presses at 3:00 a.m. A favorite and very dangerous newsie trick was to jump on and off the moving street cars, selling armloads of papers up and down the aisles. Newsies were not paid wages, but had to give circulation managers cash for their supply of papers. Since newsies had to take the loss for any papers they failed to sell, they usually worked the street corners until they sold out.

Rags to Riches: The Bootstrap Myth

During the second half of the 19th and early 20th centuries, books by Horatio Alger, Jr. (1832-1899), typically titled Bound to Rise; Making His Way; Dan, the Newsboy, Do and Dare; Brave and Bold, *and* Ragged Dick, *or* Street Life in New York with the Boot Blacks, *were enormously popular. Alger's theme was that any working class boy with good morals, who was willing to work hard and had the spunk, to try new ventures, would receive financial rewards. Hardships were only stepping stones on the road to fortune, and failure to escape poverty was simply due to lack of initiative. Alger's formula for success was known as the "bootstrap myth," and his idea that everyone will enjoy financial success if he works hard enough, became part of the American dream. In the following excerpt, Frank is left a penniless orphan, with a sister to care for, but is determined to make his own way in the world.*

Source: Horatio Alger, Jr., *The Cash Boy* (Cleveland & New York: World Syndicate Publishing Company, n.d.).

"I won't go to the poor house! I won't be penniless!...I've got hands to earn money and I'm going to try. I shall go to New York and get work, if it is only to black boots in the streets."

"With that spirit, Frank, you will stand a fair chance to succeed."

Once in the city, Frank lands a job as a "cash boy." Cash boys were hired by retail stores to carry money to the cashier's desk and return with the change. Not permitted to sit down at any time during their long work days, they made $2-$3 a week, but could earn more by delivering goods all over the city.

The Padrone System

The padrone system flourished between 1870 and the 1890s, when thousands of European children were brought to Eastern cities by profiteers who taught them to play the violin or accordion, to juggle and do acrobatics, then put them on the streets to perform. Any money tossed at these strolling musicians and acrobats by passersby had to be handed over to the padrones.

The creation of the Society for the Prevention of Cruelty to Children in 1875 helped states use legal power to put an end to the padrone system, as well as other abuses. In the selection that follows, Horatio Alger, Jr. describes the padrone racket.

Source: John Tebbel. *From Rags to Riches: Horatio Alger & the American Dream.* (New York: Macmillan, 1963), pp. 87-88; 94-96.

The evidence of malicious treatment which I have seen is unholy and must be stopped. The leaders must be punished. Why, I saw a boy fourteen years old, weighing fifty pounds, starved and weak, also mentally deficient. I met him at 10:00 p.m., afraid to go home for he had only collected 60 cents....Most of the little Italian musicians to be found on our city streets are brought from Calabria, the southern portion of Italy, where they are purchased from their parents for a fixed sum, or rate of annual payment....Even where the contract is for a limited term of years, the boys in five cases out of ten are not returned....A part, unable to bear the hardships and privations of the life upon which they enter, are swept off by death....

The little Italian musician must remain in the street till near midnight, and then, after a long and fatiguing day, he is liable to be beaten and sent to bed without his supper, unless he brings home a satisfactory sum of money.

These boys are wont to regard the padrone as above the law. His power seems to them absolute, and they never dream of any interference. And, indeed, there is some reason for their cherishing this opinion. However brutal his treatment, I know of no case where the law has stepped in to rescue the victim.

And this white slavery —for it merits no better name — is permitted by the law of two great nations. Italy is at fault in suffering this traffic in her children of tender years, and America is guilty in not interfering, as she might, to abridge the long hours of labor required of these boys, and forcing their cruel guardians to give them some instruction.

Children in the Sweatshops

The term "sweatshop" originated with the New York City garment industry, where entire families, usually recent immigrants, stitched clothing in crowded tenement rooms. After the cloth was finished and cut, pieces were given to "sweaters," to stitch together, make buttonholes, and finish by hand. Before the needle trades were unionized, workers were paid by the piece and had to buy or rent scissors, needles and sewing machines. "Sweatshop" is still used today to describe any small business with unhealthy working conditions, that demands long hours for low pay. In this selection, the poet Edwin Markham (1852-1940) describes conditions suffered by the children who worked in sweatshops.

Source: *Cosmopolitan Magazine*, January, 1907.

In unaired rooms, mothers and fathers sew by day and by night. Those in the home sweat-shop must work cheaper than those in the factory sweatshops....And children are called in from play to drive and drudge beside their elders....All the year in New York and other cities you may watch children radiating to and from such pitiful homes. Nearly any hour on the East Side of New York City you can see them — pallid boy or spindling girl —their faces dulled, their backs bent under a heavy load of garments piled on head and shoulders, the muscles of the whole frame in a long strain....Is it not a cruel civilization that allows little hearts and little shoulders to strain under these grown-up responsibilities, while in the same city, a pet cur is jeweled and pampered and aired on a fine lady's velvet lap on the beautiful boulevards?

Jacob Riis

Jacob Riis (1849-1914) emigrated from Denmark in 1870 to New York, where he became a journalist and social reformer. Through his writing and photographs, he exposed the terrible living and working conditions. Riis and Theodore Roosevelt became friends and their inspection tours through urban slums, when the future President was Police Commissioner of New York, had a significant impact upon Roosevelt's policies. Riis' book How the Other Half Lives, *(1890), shocked Ameri-*

cans and resulted in improvements in housing and child labor laws. Riis believed poverty to be the chief reason children had to go to work and thought government should take responsibility for social problems. In the following excerpts, Riis discusses the difficulty of enforcing laws for a minimum work age.

Source: Jacob Riis. "The Little Toilers," *The Children of the Poor*. New York, pp. 92-97. Found in Ruth Holland, *Mill Child: The Story of Child Labor in America*. (New York: Macmillan, Crowell-Collier & Collier-Macmillan Ltd., 1970), pp. 70-71.

The bulk of the sweater's work is done in the tenements, which the law that regulates factory labor does not reach....Ten hours is the legal work day in the factories, and nine o'clock the closing hour at the latest. Forty-five minutes at least must be allowed for dinner, and children under sixteen must not be employed unless they can read and write English; none at all under fourteen....In the tenement, the child works unchallenged from the day he is old enough to pull a thread. There is no such thing as a dinner hour; men, women, and children eat while they work, and the day is lengthened at both ends. Factory hands take their work with them at the close of the lawful day to eke out their scanty earnings by working overtime at home. Little chance on this ground for the campaign of education that alone can bring needed relief; small wonder that there are whole settlements on this East Side where English is practically an unknown tongue, though the children are both willing and anxious to learn. "When shall we find the time to learn?" one of them asked me. I owe him the answer yet....

One girl, who could not have been twelve years old, was hard at work at a sewing-machine in a Division Street shirt factory when we came in. She got up and ran the moment she saw us, but we caught her in the next room hiding behind a pile of shirts. She said at once that she was fourteen years old but "didn't work there." She "just came in." ...There were three boys at work in the room who said "sixteen" without waiting to be asked. Not one of them was fourteen. The habit of saying fourteen or sixteen — the fashion varies with the shops and with the degree of the child's education....

The Child-Savers

When the National Child Labor Committee was organized, its founders published a "List of Standards," which summarized its minimum demands and expectations regarding child labor.

Source: Ruth Holland, *ibid.*, p. 124.

---

1. No child under fourteen is to be employed at any job.
2. No children over fourteen shall be permitted to work more than eight hours day in a day or six days in a week.
3. No children shall be permitted to do any kind of night work.
4. No children shall be employed in the dangerous trades or any work that might possibly do harm to their health.
5. No child will be permitted employment anywhere without first obtaining a work permit proving his/her age beyond any doubt.
6. No child shall be employed while school is in session unless he or she has completed the eighth grade.

Jane Addams of Hull-House

In 1889, Jane Addams (1860-1935) purchased a building in the Chicago slums and established Hull House, a community center that offered day-care, English classes, cooking lessons, health education, a boys' club, concerts, theater, and a labor museum, among other programs. It became the prototype for settlement houses all over the country, that served the urban immigrant population. Addams' campaign against child labor resulted in the Illinois Factory Act of 1893, one of the earliest attempts to regulate the hours and safety of children in the workplace. In the following selection Addams expresses her shock when first becoming aware of the abuses of child labor.

Source: Jane Addams, "Pioneer Labor Legislation in Illinois, 1910," *A Centennial Reader*, (NY: Macmillan, 1960), pp. 192-194.

Our very first Christmas at Hull-House, when we as yet knew nothing of child labor, a number of little girls refused candy offered them as part of the Christmas good cheer, saying they "worked in a candy factory and could not bear the sight of it." We discovered that for six weeks they had worked from seven in the morning until nine at night, and were exhausted as well as satiated. The sharp consciousness of stern economic conditions was thus thrust upon us in the midst of the season of good will.

During the same winter three boys from a Hull-House club were injured at one machine in a neighboring factory for lack of a guard rail which would have cost but a few dollars. When the injury of one of these boys resulted in his death, we felt quite sure that the owners of the factory would share our horror and would do everything possible to prevent the recurrence of such a tragedy. To our surprise they did nothing whatever, and I made my first acquaintance then with those pathetic documents signed by parents of working children, that they will make no claim for damages resulting from carelessness....We came to know many families in which working children contributed to the support of their parents, not only because they spoke English better than the older immigrants and were willing to take lower wages, but because the parent gradually found it easy to live upon their child's earnings.

In the following excerpt, Jane Addams shares her concerns over the unhealthy and dangerous conditions working children were forced to endure, and suggests some solutions to the problems.

Source: Jane Addams, *80 Years at Hull-House.* Allen F. Davis & Mary Lynn McCree, Editors. (Chicago: Quadrangle, 1968), p. 48.

The largest number of children to be found in any one factory in Chicago is in a caramel works in this ward, where there are from 110 to 200 little girls, four to twelve boys, and 70 to 100 adults, according to the season of the year....The building has no fire-escape, and a single wooden stair leading from floor to floor. In case of fire the inevitable fate of the children working on the two upper floors is too horrible to contemplate. The box factory is on the fifth floor, and the heaviest pressure of steam used in boiling the caramels is all on the top floor. The little girls sit closely packed at long tables, wrapping and packing caramels. They are paid by the piece, and the number of pennies per thousand paid is just enough to attract the most ignorant and helpless children.

Previous to the passage of the factory law of 1893, it was the rule of this factory to work the children, for several weeks before the Christmas holidays from 7 a.m. to 9 p.m., with 20 minutes for lunch, and no supper, a working week of 82 hours. As this overtime season coincided with the first term of the night school, the children lost their one opportunity. Since the enactment of the factory law, their working week has consisted of six days of eight hours each; a reduction of 34 hours a week....

It is a lamentable fact, well known to those who have investigated child-labor, that children are found in greatest number where the conditions of labor are most dangerous to life and health. Among the occupations in which children are most employed in Chicago, and which most endanger the health, are: the tobacco trade, nicotine poisoning finding as many victims among factory children as among the boys who are voluntary devotees of the weed, consumers of the deadly cigarette included; frame gilding, in which work a child's fingers are stiffened and throat disease is contracted; button-holing, machine-stitching, and hand-work in tailor or sweatshops, the machine-work producing spinal curvature, and for girls pelvic disorders also, while the unsanitary condition of the shops makes even hand-sewing dangerous; bakeries, where children slowly roast before the ovens; binderies, paper-box and paint factories, where arsenic paper, rotting paste, and the poison of the paints are injurious; boiler-plate works, cutlery works, and metal-stamping works, where the dust produces lung disease; the handling of hot metal, accidents; the hammering of plate, deafness. In addition to diseased incidental to trades, there are the conditions of bad sanitation and long hours, almost universal in the factories where children are employed....

The key to the child-labor question is the enforcement of school attendance to the age of sixteen, and the granting of help to the poorest of the working children as shall make our public schools not class institutions, but indeed and in truth, the schools of the people, by the people, for the people. Only when every child is known to be in school can there be any security against the tenement-house labor of children in our great cities.

The legislation needed is of the simplest description:

1) the minimum age for work fixed at sixteen
2) School attendance made compulsory to the same age
3) Factory inspectors and truant officers...charged with the duty of removing children from mill and workshop, mine and store, and placing them at school.
4) Ample provision for school accommodations; money supplied by the State through school authorities for the support of such orphans, half-orphans, and children of the unemployed as are now kept out of school by destitution.

Where they are, the wage-earning children are an unmitigated injury to themselves, to the community upon which they will later be burdens, and to the trade which they demoralize. They learn nothing valuable; they shorten the average of the trade life, and they lower the standard of living of the adults with whom they compete.

..."if they are old enough to stand"

In this selection Edith Abbott, a social reformer who lived at Chicago's Hull-House, recorded an example of the disregard of child labor laws by some employers.

Source: Edith Abbott. "Child Labor in America Before 1870," in *Women in Industry: A Study in American Economic History.* (New York, London: Appleton, 1910), from MA Legislature House Document No. 98, "Report of the Special Committee on the Hours of Labor and the Condition and Prospects of the Industrial Classes," February 1866, pp. 345-346.

Mill manager from Fall River, MA:

Small help is scarce. A great deal of the machinery has been stopped for want of small help, so the overseers have been going round to draw the small children from the schools into the mills; the same as a draft in the army.

Question (from state congressman): Do I understand agents go about to take children out of schools and put them into mills?

Answer: They go round to the parents and canvass them....The boys and girls are mixed up together from seven years up to thirteen and are entirely demoralized.

Question: How old are the children?

Answer: Seven and eight.

Question: Have you a child of seven working in the mills?

Answer: Yes, I have.

Question: Does he get any schooling now?

Answer: When he gets done the mill he is ready to go to bed. He has to be in the mill ten minutes before we start up to wind spindles. Then he starts about his own work and keeps on till dinner time. Then he goes home, starts again at one o'clock and works till seven. When he's done he's tired enough to go to bed. Some days he has to clean and help scour during dinner hour....Saturdays, he's in all day.

Question: Is there any limit on the part of employers as to the age when the take children?

Answer: They'll take them at any age they can get them, if they are old enough to stand.

"Turn all working children into school children!"

Florence Kelley (1853-1932) was determined to "turn all working children into school children." Another resident of Hull House, she became Chief Factory Inspector for Illinois in 1893. She later served as secretary to the National Federation of Consumer Leagues, which provided a political platform for her continuing crusade against child labor. When Florence Kelley addressed the third annual meeting of the National Child Labor Committee in 1906, numerous laws had already been passed that prohibited the hiring of children in certain occupations or limited their working hours. In the selection that follows, Kelley pointed out some reasons why these laws were not being enforced and proposed ways to strengthen them.

Source: "Obstacles to Enforcing Child Labor Laws" *The Annals of America*, Vol. 13, 1905-1915. Encyclopedia Britannica Publishing Company, 1968, pp. 85-89.

...the great manufacturers say: "There is no child labor in this country. If there were, it would be a bad thing. We do not employ young children. This is all exaggeration." But they do employ children, and the children are working tonight. I know that children six, seven, and eight years old work this week in New York City tenements for reputable manufacturers. I have seen children in a cotton mill in Georgia whose employer told me they were twelve years old, who were wretched dwarfs if they were really eight years old...the entire attitude of the manufacturing class has been revolutionized in sixty years....

There are three objective tests of the enforcement of our laws. One is the presence of children in school....In 1904, when the present child labor law of Illinois had taken effect, the enrollment in the Chicago schools of children of compulsory school age tripled....That statute carried 1,000 children out of the stockyards in a single week; and it carried 2,200 children out of the mines of Illinois in another week....

The second objective test of the enforcement of child labor laws is prosecution....Hundreds of employers have paid thousands of dollars in fines, and the visible result of the success of those prosecutions is the presence of the children of compulsory school age in school....South of Baltimore-south of Louisville — there are no prosecutions; there is no compulsory school attendance....There are few blacker chapters in the history of this Republic than the ever recurring story of removal of efficient officers because they have attempted to enforce child labor laws in communities which were willing to have those laws on the statute books so long as they were not enforced, but either repealed the statutes or removed the officers as soon as there was any effective prosecution....

The third test of the enforcement of the child labor laws is the published records of the officials appointed to enforce them. The friends of the children are growing in numbers, but they often lack technical acquaintance with the subject. It may be said of many of us that our intentions are good, but we have never been working children; we have never been employers; we have perhaps, never been teachers of working children, and we do not speak with authority....

These, I believe, are the gravest obstacles to the enforcement of the child labor law: first, the general hypocrisy of the American people, believing that child labor is an evil, and therefore, we do not tolerate it — when there are working children on the streets before our eyes, every working day in the year, in every manufacturing city; second, the failure to make the work of enforcing the law a desirable and recognized profession into which the ablest men will willingly go....In America, we leave an inspector at the mercy of the most influential man whom it may be his duty to prosecute, and at the mercy of every turn of the political wheel....And we fall to thinking that there is something hopeless in the effort to put better laws upon the statute book if then they are to sleep upon its pages.

...The next step which we need to take is to insist that this is a national evil, and we must have a national law abolishing it. We must also insist that this is a matter of great importance to the people of this country, that the government must give us information through a bureau for the children in the federal government....

Crusader With A Camera: Lewis Wickes Hine

These jobs involve work, hard work, deadening in its monotony, exhausting physically....We might even say of these children that they are condemned to work.

— Lewis W. Hine

The child-savers needed documentary proof so the American public would understand the abuses they were fighting to correct, as well as to prove that child labor laws were being broken. The National Child Labor Committee hired Lewis W. Hine (1874-1940) to photograph children at work and to record their stories. Working for the NCLC from 1907 through 1913, Hine logged some 50,000 miles a year. He stayed in workers' homes, camped in fields, and often developed his glass-plate negatives in coal bins. Hine said this exploitation of children was nothing less than "Making Human Junk."

Source: Russell Freedman. *Kids At Work: Lewis Hine and the Crusade Against Child Labor.* Illustrated with Hine's photographs. (New York: Clarion Books, 1994), p. 26.

Factory managers frequently tried to keep Hine out, for they did not want something as profitable as child labor exposed to the public. To gain entry into factories and mines, Hine often pretended to be a fire inspector, salesman, or an engineer sent in to check machines. Then he would ask a small worker to pose beside a machine, saying he needed to show scale in his photos. If he could not get inside, he would set up his camera outside to photograph children coming and going to their jobs. The selec-

tions that follow represent some examples of Hine's observations which he recorded as photo captions.

Augusta, Georgia - Entrance to the mill was extremely difficult. The man in charge absolutely refused to let me through, even as a visitor. So I waited close outside the main gate, concealed in the darkness of the woods, and at 6:00 p.m., I counted about 35 boys who appeared to be from 9 to 14 years of age. I stopped them and took them around the corner for a flash-powder photo. Some of the smallest said they had been working at the mill several years.

Bells, Texas 1913 - Photographed tiny bits of humanity, picking cotton in every field....In the cotton fields of this farm children as young as four or five are picking cotton. A large portion of all the cotton is said to be picked by children under fourteen. The very young children like to pick at first, but before long they detest it. The sun is hot, the hours long, and the bags heavy.

New York City - Photographed a family around the kitchen table making paper flowers by light of kerosene lamp. Angelica is 3 years old. She pulls apart the petals, inserts the center, and glues it to the stem, making 540 flowers a day for 5 cents.

Source: Lewis Hine. *Child Labor Bulletin*, 1914. Found in *America and Lewis Hine: Photographs 1904-1940; A Retrospective of the Photographer Lewis W. Hine*. (New York: An Aperture Monograph, 1977).

For many years I have followed the procession of child workers winding through a thousand industrial communities from the canneries of Maine to the fields of Texas. I have heard their tragic stories, watched their cramped lives and seen their fruitless struggles in the industrial game where the odds are all against them. I wish I could give you a bird's eye view of my varied experience.

Mother Jones:
"The Most Dangerous Woman in America"

To most workers, Mary Harris Jones (1830-1930), an Irish immigrant, was "The Miners' Angel," but many others called her the "most dangerous woman in America." After the deaths of her husband and four children in a Memphis yellow fever epidemic, she moved to Chicago to open a dressmaking shop, but that was destroyed in the Great Chicago Fire. When she saw workers shot down by militiamen during the railroad strikes of 1877, she was determined to devote all her energies to the labor cause. For the rest of her long life, she roamed the country as a union organizer, speaking and writing on behalf of human rights.

The Children's Crusade

Sixteen thousand of the 100,000 workers who went on strike at the Kensington Textile Mills outside Philadelphia in 1903 were children. Although Pennsylvania had passed a law forbidding anyone under thirteen to work in mills, only a parent's signature was required to certify the child's age. Summoned to Kensington from the West Virginia mining camps, Mother Jones was appalled when she saw that most youngsters at the strikers' meeting were only nine or ten. In this excerpt, the labor leader recalls her horror at seeing that some of the children were missing fingers.

Source: Mary Harris Jones. *Autobiography of Mother Jones*, Mary Field Parton, editor, (Chicago: Charles H. Kerr, 1925). Found in Linda Atkinson, *Mother Jones: The Most Dangerous Woman in America*. (New York: Crown, 1978), p. 118.

I held up their mutilated hands — some with fingers off, some whose bones had been crushed and made the statement that Philadelphia's mansions were built on the broken bones, the quivering hearts and drooping heads of these children; that their little lives went out to make wealth for others....

On July 7, 1903, three hundred men, women, and children, led by Mother Jones, set off from Philadelphia to President Theodore Roosevelt's home at Oyster Bay, Long Island. The children, some dressed as "The Spirit of 1776," carried banners with slogans: "We Only Ask for Justice;" "More Schools, Less Hospitals;" "We Want to Go to School! We Want Time to Play." They marched about ten miles each day and were provided food and shelter by sympathizers along the way. As they passed through each town, the children performed plays and entertained crowds with music, and their leader would speak. Following is an excerpt from a speech Mother Jones gave July 28, 1903, at Coney Island, Brooklyn, New York.

Source: Philip S. Foner, editor. *Mother Jones Speaks: Collected Writings & Speeches.* (New York: Monad Press, 1983), pp. 102-133.

After a long and weary march, with more miles to travel, we are on our way to see President Roosevelt. We will ask him to recommend passage of a bill by Congress to protect children against the greed of the manufacturer. We want him to hear the wail of the children, who never have a chance to go to school, but work from ten to eleven hours a day in textile mills, weaving the carpets that he and you walk on, and the curtains and clothes of the people.

Fifty years ago there was a cry against slavery, and the men of the North gave up their lives to stop the selling of black children on the block. Today the white child is sold for $2 a week, and even by his parents, to the manufacturer. Fifty years ago, black babies were sold C.O.D. Today the white baby is sold to the manufacturer on the installment plan. He might die at his tasks and the manufacturer with his automobile and yacht and the daughter who talks French to a poodle dog, cannot afford to pay $2 a week for the child who might die....What the President can do is recommend a measure and send a message to Congress which will break the chains of these white children slaves....You are told that every American-born male citizen has a chance of being President. I tell you that these little toilers, deformed, dwarfed in body, soul, and morality, with nothing but toil before them and no chance for schooling, don't even have the dream that they might some day have a chance at the Presidential chair....We are going to tell the President of these things.

Mother Jones Writes President "Teddy" Roosevelt

The 26th President's Message to Congress included the elimination of child labor abuses and during the administration of Theodore Roosevelt, 1901-1909, many states did pass new laws regulating age and restricting the number of hours that children could legally work. Mother Jones was convinced that once the President saw these mill children, he would offer the federal government's support. Following is an excerpt from one of her letters to Roosevelt.

Source: Foner, Ed. *ibid.*, pp. 552-555.

New York, July 30, 1903

Your Excellency:

Twice before have I written you requesting an audience that I might lay my mission before you and have your advice on a matter which bears upon the welfare of the whole nation. I speak for the emancipation from mills and factories of the hundreds of thousands of young children who are yielding up their lives for the commercial supremacy of the nation. Failing to receive a reply to my letters, I yesterday went to Oyster Bay, taking with me three of the children that they might plead to you personally....It was for them that our march of principle was begun. We sought to bring the attention of the public upon these little ones, so that sentiment would be aroused and the children freed from workshops and sent to school....The child of today is the man or woman of tomorrow....I ask Mr. President, what kind of citizen will be the child who toils twelve hours a day, in an unsanitary atmosphere, stunted mentally and physically, and surrounded with immoral influences? Denied education, he cannot assume the true duties of citizenship, and enfeebled physically and mentally, he falls a ready victim to the perverting influences which the present economic conditions have created.

I grant you, Mr. President, that there are State laws which should regulate these matters, but results have proven that they are inadequate. In my little band are three boys, the oldest 11 years, who have been working in mills a year or more without interference from the authorities. All efforts to bring about reform have failed.

I have been moved to this crusade, Mr. President, because of actual experience in the mills. I have seen little children without the first rudiments of education and no prospect of acquiring any. I have seen other children with hands, fingers and other parts of their tiny bodies mutilated because of their childish ignorance of machinery. I feel that no nation can be truly great while such conditions exist without attempted remedy....I believe that Federal laws should be passed governing this evil and including a penalty for violation....

Two factory girls at a hosiery mill in Tennessee, by Lewis Hine
(Library of Congress)

President Roosevelt failed to respond. Mother Jones and her marchers were stopped at Roosevelt's gate by his secretary, who said the President "might have been willing to meet with her" *had she* "made a formal request through the White House," *but Theodore Roosevelt* "did not like having his castle stormed." *Secretary Barnes explained that* "the children had the President's heartfelt sympathy, as shown by the anti-child labor act passed when he was Governor of New York, but that under the Constitution, Congress had no power to act....The states alone have the power to deal with this subject."

Different Points of View

Many believed child labor "beneficial to society." Mill and mine managers who regularly hired children said that children who worked "kept their parents from depending upon charity." They insisted it was the "child's right to work; work kept children out of trouble and made them healthy and happy." Child labor also kept production costs down and increased profits. Examples of some different points of view follow.

Source: William Cahn. *Pictorial History of American Labor: The Contributions of the Working Men & Women to America's Growth, from Colonial Times to the Present.* (New York: Crown, 1972), p. 194.

My little workers seem to be always cheerful and alert, taking pleasure in the light play of their muscles; enjoying the mobility natural to their age....The work of these lively elves seemed to resemble a sport in which habit gave them a pleasing dexterity.

— A textile employer, 1900

* * * * * * * * *

The most beautiful sight that we see is the child at labor. As early as he may get at labor the more beautiful, the more useful does his life get to be.

— Asa G. Caudler
founder of the Coca Cola Company

* * * * * * * * *

They have to be constantly watched or they will go from bad to worse in order to make more time for play.

— *Textile World Magazine*

* * * * * * * * *

Source: Katharine Du Pre Lumpkin & Dorothy Wolff Douglas. *Child Workers in America*. (NY: Robert M. McBride, 1937), p. 219.

The dangers of child idleness are as great or greater than the dangers of child labor. If laws raised the minimum working age, companies would have to replace children with more expensive adults and that would reduce profits. If such child labor laws are passed, the morals of the children are going to be corrupted because they would be allowed to loaf around the street.

— Owner of a Southern textile mill, 1910

* * * * * * * * *

Source: *National Conference of Social Work for the National Child Labor Committee*, June 12, 1925. Found in Ronald Taylor. *Sweatshops in the Sun: Child Labor On the Farm*. (Boston: Beacon Press, 1973), p. 1.

The real problem in America is not child labor, but child idleness. You cannot convince me that it hurts a child either physically or morally to make him work. Where one child, in my experience, has been injured from work, ten thousand have gone to the devil because of lack of occupation....

— Senator Charles S. Thomas, 1925

* * * * * * * * *

John Mitchell, president of the United Mine Workers union from 1898 to 1908, represents a different point of view. He had once been a child laborer in the coal mines.

Source: William Cahn, *op. cit.*, p. 194.

...It is hard to reconcile the humanity and intelligence of this era with the wholesale employment of children in industry. Childhood should be a period of growth and education. It should be the stage in which the man is trained for future efforts and future work....It is difficult to conceive of anything more utterly absurd and immoral, than the wholesale employment of children....The policy of extracting work from children and exploiting their slow-growing strength is utterly vicious and entirely self-destructive....

Samuel Gompers on Child Labor

Trade unions consistently took a stand against child labor, believing a man's wages ought be high enough so that his wife and children would not have to work. Union leaders were convinced that hiring children kept adult wages down. The excerpt that follows comes from a speech delivered by Samuel Gompers (1850-1924), president of the American Federation of Labor (AF of L) in 1888.

Source: Samuel Gompers. *"Seventy Years of Life and Labor" An Autobiography.* (New York: Dutton, 1925; 1943), pp. 225-226.

Some of you may be tempted to send your children out to work. That may seem a very grateful addition to the income. But don't you know that the child is employed because its labor can be had cheaper than that of a man? He becomes a competitor of his father. And if the father is not discharged, some other child's father often is. In this competition, the rates of labor are often so reduced that the combined wages of the father and child are less than the father's wages before....It is bad even from an economic point of view to send young children out to work.

Kids on Strike

The earliest recorded strike led by children, took place in 1828 in Paterson, New Jersey, when a factory changed its employees' dinner hour. The children marched out of the mill, cheered on by fellow workers. Soon joined by adult workers, the children's walk-out became a general strike for the ten-hour workday.

Harriet Hanson Robinson (1824-1911), the daughter of a boarding housekeeper, was ten when she went to work in a Lowell factory. Except for three months off each year to attend school, as required by Massachusetts law, she spent the next thirteen years as a millgirl. In the following selection, Robinson recalls her role as a strike leader at the age of eleven.

Source: Harriet Hanson Robinson. *Loom and Spindle or Life Among the Early Mill Girls.* Originally published 1898.

One of the first strikes of cotton-factory operatives that ever took place in this country was in Lowell, in October, 1836. When it was announced that wages were to be cut, great indignation was felt, and it was decided to strike, en masse....The mills were shut down, and the girls went in procession from several corporations to listen to speeches from labor reformers....It was estimated that as many as 1500 girls turned out....I worked in a lower room, where I had heard the proposed strike fully, if not vehemently, discussed; I had been an ardent listener to what was said against this attempt at "oppression" on the part of the corporation, and naturally, I took sides with the strikers. When the day came on which the girls were to turn out, those in the upper rooms started first, and so many of them left that our mill was at once shut down. Then, when the girls in my room stood uncertain what to do, asking each other, "Would you?" or "Shall we turn out?" and not one of them having the courage to lead off, I, who began to think they would not go out after all their talk, became impatient, and started on ahead, saying, with childish bravado, "I don't care what you do, I am going to turn out, whether any one else does or not!" and I marched out, and was followed by the others.

As I looked back at the long line that followed me, I was more proud than I have ever been since at any success I may have achieved....The agent of the corporation where I then worked took some small revenges on the supposed ringleaders; on the principle of sending the weaker to the wall, my mother was turned away from her boarding house, "Mrs. Hanson, you could not prevent the older girls from turning out, but your daughter is a child, and her you could control!"

Strike of the Newsies

Newsies made their own headlines in the summer of 1899. When publishers William Randolph Hearst and Joseph Pulitzer raised distribution prices on their newspapers, the newsies formed a union and went on strike. The streets of New York were filled with noisy demonstrations and newsies carrying signs which read, "Our Cause Is Just; We Will Fight For Our Rights!" and "Don't Buy The World or Journal!" The strike continued until mid-August, when Hearst and Pulitzer, admitting "loss in circulation had been colossal," negotiated to settle the strike. Prices would remain the same but the publishers would take back any newspapers which the newsies could not sell with full refunds. The following section shows how a rival newspaper reported this strike.
Source: *New York Times*, July 26, 1899.

NEWSBOYS STILL HOLD OUT
Strikers Pass a More Quiet Day and Few Fights Are Reported

The newsboys' strike against *The Evening World* and *Evening Journal* was of a less bellicose nature yesterday than it had been on Monday, and the men and big boys who had been hired to sell the papers were attacked in only a few instances. Five men went to sell the papers at 125th Street and Third Avenue, and were surrounded by a mob of strikers. The opposing factions held a parley, which ended in a conditional truce for the day. The men were allowed to sell their papers to whoever asked for them, but they were not to call their wares nor to thrust them under the noses of passers-by. These two privileges of the trade the strikers reserved for themselves exclusively. At 8th Avenue and 125th Street several men were found selling the papers, and they defied the strikers when ordered to desist. Just as the boys were about to attack the men several policemen swooped down on them and scattered them by a few light blows of their clubs. The boys hid around the corners, and as soon as the policemen were out of sight they attacked the men and took away their papers and tore them up.

Having served its purpose, the union did not last, yet the victory of the New York newsies started what journalists called a "strike epidemic." Bootblacks and messenger boys joined newsies in calling strikes. While the "New York Times" generally supported the strikers, the following item from a Cincinnati newspaper expresses an opposing point of view regarding the strike of telegraph messengers in their city. "New messengers," workers hired by the company to take the place of the striking boys, were called "scabs" by sympathizers.

MESSENGER BOYS RIDE IN CABS
Police Cannot Keep Cincinnati Hoodlums from Attacking Them

CINCINNATI, Ohio, July 25 - The strike of messenger boys that began last Saturday has reached serious conditions. Hoodlums and idlers to-day surrounded the telegraph and district offices in different parts of the city, and intercepted the new messengers. The messengers were sent out in cabs with a policeman accompanying each driver, but stones and missiles were thrown at the vehicles. Many of the messengers have been seriously hurt. Two have been stabbed, several hurt by missiles, and many have been badly beaten.

The newsboys joined in the strike to-day. Great mobs of hoodlums surrounded the newspaper offices and refused to let the news boys go out with papers. The papers were torn up and destroyed as fast as they were turned over to the new boys. At noon the hoodlums from all parts of the city had gathered in such large numbers that the police seemed unable to disperse them with clubs, and the use of more effective weapons was contemplated.

Camella Teoli's Testimony

In 1912, half of the children who lived in Lawrence, Massachusetts worked in its textile mills and 169 out of every thousand died each year. When a new state law to shorten the work day went into effect in January, mill owners also cut wages. For families living on a pittance, 32 cents could mean doing without bread. United across language and ethnic barriers, 20,000 workers went out on strike.

Camella Teoli, a daughter of Italian immigrants, was one of sixteen child strikers who travelled to Washington in March, 1912 to testify before Congress. First Lady Helen Taft was present the day Camella told her story and spearheaded an investigation of workers' conditions all over the country.

Source: *Hearings on Committee of Rules, House of Representatives*, Document #671, 62nd Congress, 2nd Session, Washington, D. C., March 2-7, 1912.

Chairman: Camella, how old are you?

Camella Teoli: Fourteen years and eight months.

Chairman: How many children are there in your family?

Camella: Five

Chairman: Where do you work?

Camella: In the American Woolen Company

Chairman: What sort of work do you do?

Camella: Twisting

Chairman: How much do you get in a week?

Camella: $6.55

Chairman: What is the smallest pay?

Camella: $2.64

Chairman: Do you have to pay for water?

Camella: Yes. Ten cents every two weeks

Chairman: Does your father work, and if so, where?

Camella: My father works in the Washington Woolen Mill.

Chairman: How much does he get for a week's work?

Camella: $7.70

Chairman: How often does it happen that he does not work a full week?

Camella: He works in winter a full week, and usually he don't work in the summer but two or three days a week....

Chairman: Now, did you ever get hurt in the mill?

Camella: Yes.

Chairman: Can you tell us about it now in your own way?

Camella: Well, I used to go to school, and then a man came up to my house and asked my father why I didn't go to work, so my father says I don't know whether she is 13 or 14 years old. So, the man say you give me $4.00, and I will make the papers come from the old country saying she is 14. So, my father gave him $4. 00, and in one month came the papers that said I was 14. I went to work, and after about two weeks got hurt in my head.

49

Chairman: Now, how did you get hurt, and where were you hurt in the head? Explain that to the Committee.

Camella: I got hurt in the Washington Mill....

Chairman: Well, how were you hurt?

Camella: The machine pulled the scalp off.

Chairman: The machine pulled your scalp off?

Camella: Yes, sir.

Chairman: How long ago was that?

Camella: About a year ago.

Chairman: Were you in the hospital after that?

Camella: I was in the hospital seven months.

Chairman: Did the company take care of you? Pay your wages?

Camella: The company only paid my hospital bills. They didn't give me anything else....

Chairman: Did they arrest your father for having sent you to work for fourteen?

Camella: Yes, sir.

Chairman: What did they do with him after they arrested him?

Camella: My father told about the man he gave $4. 00 to, and then they let him on again.

Chairman: Are you still being treated by the doctors for your scalp wound?

Camella: Yes, sir.

Chairman: How much longer do they tell you that you will have to be treated?

Camella: They don't know.

Chairman: Are you working now?

Camella: Yes, sir.

Chairman: How much are you getting?

Camella: $6.55

Chairman: Are you working in the same place where you were before you were hurt?

Camella: No, in another mill. The Wood Mill....

Chairman: How long did you go to school?

Camella: I left when I was in the sixth grade.

Chairman: And have you been working ever since except while you were in the hospital?

Camella: Yes, sir.

Mr. Campbell: Do you know the man who came to your father and offered to get a certificate saying that you were fourteen years of age?

Camella: I know the man, but I have forgot him now....

Mr. Campbell: You are sure he was connected or employed by some of the mills?

Camella: I don't know. I don't think so.

Mr. Campbell: Did he ever come about your house visiting there? I mean before he asked about your going to work in the mills?

Camella: Yes, sir....

Mr. Campbell: Do they go around in Lawrence there and find little girls and boys in schools over fourteen years of age and urge them to quit school and go to work in the mills?

Camella: No. I don't know.

Mr. Campbell: Do you know any little girls besides yourself, who were asked to go to work as soon as they were fourteen?

Camella: No, I don't know.

Mr. Hardwick: Are you one of the strikers?

Camella: Yes, sir.

Mr. Hardwick: Did you agree to strike before it was ordered? Did they ask you about striking before you quit?

Camella: No.

Mr. Hardwick: But you joined them after they quit?

Camella: Yes.

Mr. Hardwick: Why did you do that?

Camella: Because I didn't get enough to eat at home.

Junior Unions

The following sections are from an article published by McClure's *in 1903, in which the author described unions organized by children working for Pennsylvania mining companies.*

Source: William Cahn, *op. cit.*, pp. 193-195.

The members of the Junior Local are all boys under sixteen. Their weekly meetings take place at night, and are conducted with the utmost secrecy, members being admitted only by pass-word. Monthly dues range from 10 to 25 cents, in accordance with the wages received by members....I attended a meeting of a Junior Local....Comparatively few of the members who filled benches in the room would have been pronounced by any observer as being more than ten years of age.

"How old are you?" I asked the assembled meeting, and the answer came back in a grand chorus. "Thirteen." An accord of ideas, as well as ages, worthy of a union.

....

Just as the boys in the mines had junior locals, so did their sisters.....The debates were about wages and hours and working conditions. Often the discussions led to serious action, strikes. The girls asserted themselves almost as often and with almost as much strength as the dirty, grimy miners. Sometimes an injustice done to one girl would arouse the feelings of her sisters.

One strike was called when a very little girl began to grow crippled from operating a treadle. She became so lame and ill that she had to stay home for a week and go to bed. During that time a large boy was hired to do her work. He was, of course, paid more money. When the girl returned, the boy was fired and the girl put back on the treadle. The boss refused to find other work for her. In the words of a young union leader, "Shall we stand for it, girls, for seeing her grow up a cripple and the union not doing nothing, not reaching out no hand for to help? We that believes in the rights of man?" Some had fathers who were striking, but the vote was unanimous.

"We had the resolution to strike written out nice on a typewriter," the leader said. After two days the boss gave in. The boy worked at the treadle and the girl was placed at work at a bench.

Child Laborers of Stage and Screen

"An Act to Keep Children Off the Stage"

As the rate of child employment continued to rise, the Knights of Labor and other unions pushed harder for state regulations. Some states passed legislation against certain occupations as "moral wrongs to children." The excerpt which follows comes from a New York law that prohibited the employment of children in musical and theatrical productions.

Source: "General Statutes of New York," Chapter 122, 1876. *Annals of America*, #80, 1876, pp. 353-354.

Section 1: Any person having the care, custody, or control of any child under the age of sixteen who shall exhibit, use, or employ, or who shall in any manner or under any pretense sell, apprentice, give away, let out, or otherwise dispose of any such child to any person in or for the vocation, occupation, service, or purpose of singing, playing on musical instruments, rope or wire walking, dancing, begging or peddling, or as a gymnast, contortionist, rider, or acrobat, in any place whatsoever; or for or in any obscene, indecent, or immoral purpose, exhibition, or practice whatsoever; or for or in any business, exhibition, or vocation injurious to the health or dangerous to the life or limb of such child; or who shall cause, procure, or encourage any such child to engage therein, shall be guilty of a misdemeanor....Nothing in this section shall apply to or affect the employment or use of any such child as a singer or musician in any church, school, or academy, of the teaching or learning the science or practice of music; nor the employment of any child as a musician at any concert or entertainment, on the written consent of the mayor of the city....

Section 2: Every person who shall take, receive, hire, employ, use, exhibit, or have in custody any child under the age, and for any of the purposes mentioned in the 1st Section of this act shall be guilty of a misdemeanor....

Kids At Work In Hollywood

Robert Blake, born Mickey Gubitosi, in 1933, sang and danced on stage from the age of two. He appeared in forty "Our Gang" comedies and played the Mexican boy in the 1947 classic, "Treasure of Sierra Madre." In the 1940s, he was "Little Beaver" in the Red Ryder series. After some difficult years with substance abuse, Blake made a comeback in films like "In Cold Blood." He won an Emmy for his TV series "Baretta."

Source: Leonard Maltin and Richard W. Bann. *Our Gang: The Life & Times of The Little Rascals.* (NY: Crown, 1977), pp. 274-275.

I wasn't a child star. I was a child laborer. In the morning, my mother would deliver me to the MGM Studio like a dog on a leash....I was like most child performers. I acted only because I was told to. I didn't like it. It was no kind of life. Forcing a kid to become a performer is one of the worst things that can happen to a child. It's turning them into adults when they're still youngsters.

Jackie Cooper was a Hollywood star at eight, appearing in many "Our Gang" shorts. In 1931, he captured America's heart as the prizefighter's son in "The Champ." He appeared in "The Newsboys' Home" and "Streets of New York" in 1939, but found roles rarer when he was no longer a cute, freckle-faced kid. Later, he starred in two television series, "The People's Choice" and "Hennessey," and eventually became a successful television producer and director. He received an Emmy as director of "Mash" episodes.

Source: *Please Don't Shoot My Dog:* The Autobiography of Jackie Cooper, with Dick Kleiner. (New York: William Morrow, 1981), pp. 37-38.

The longer I stayed on the set, the less time I had to spend in school....There were no laws then about taking it easy on kids-those came later — so we worked from eight in the morning until six at night like everybody else. But I never minded the work. It was make-believe....So I'd go in and out of grammar school....When I was working, I didn't have to go....I didn't know that back there in the schoolyard, normal kids were having normal, and much healthier, fun.

Later, people tried to rationalize to me that I had gained more than I lost by being a child star. They talked to me about the money I had made. They cited the exciting things I had done, the people I had met, the career training I had....But no amount of rationalization, no excuses, can make up for what a kid loses — what I lost — when a normal childhood is abandoned for an early movie career....I'm talking about the child who grows up empty and doesn't realize it until it's too late. I'm talking about me. I gained a lot...money, experiences, career — but think of what I lost. I had no friends. That deprived me of the early competition which I have discovered is so valuable in the growing-up process. I did not receive a good education. Tutors on the set can be manipulated by a street-smart kid and a succession of directors who just want to get the work done and the hell with the kid's education. For many adult years, I had trouble reading because I simply wasn't properly trained.

I grew up with pressure and responsibility. Most children don't experience them until they are teenagers, if then. I had it from the time I was seven or eight. The pressure to get the scene right, to learn the words, to act this way or that way, to smile or cry or look scared for the camera-man, to do a nice interview. The responsibility to work correctly for the director who tells you that if you don't do a good job, he may get fired and he has three little babies at home to feed. Why should an eight year old kid have to have that kind of pressure?

The Coogan Act or Child Actor's Bill

Source: Edward Edelson. *Great Kids of the Movies*. (Garden City, New York: Doubleday, 1979, p. 37); also "Parental Greed," *American History Magazine*, February 1997, p. 42.

Readers may remember Jackie Coogan as "Uncle Fester" in "The Addams Family." Born in 1914 to Vaudeville parents, he was a stage performer from the age of two. Charlie Chaplin gave him the title role in his 1921 film "The Kid," and the boy was an overnight sensation. Jackie was soon earning between $5,000 and $10,000 per week. When he turned twenty-one and tried to claim some of the $4 million dollars he had earned as a child, Coogan learned that

This magnificent car and home in Los Angeles were purchased by Jackie Coogan's parents with some of the $4 million he earned as a child star. Young Jackie is standing on the running board. The extensive lawsuits that followed led to the passing of the Coogan Act, protecting the interests of child wage-earners. (Library of Congress)

he had no legal right to it. He sued his mother and stepfather to win back his salary, but by law, any money earned by minors belonged to the parents. The court battle continued many years, costing thousands in legal fees. Coogan finally settled out of court but when he died in 1984, he was still fighting for passage of a law that would force parents of child performers to set up trust funds for underage wage earners.

As a result of the Coogan case, the California State Legislature passed the "Child Actors Bill." This decreed that at least fifty percent of a child's earnings be set aside in a trust fund or some form of court-approved savings plan, until the child reached eighteen. This law is still considered weak since it only covers long-term film contracts and television series.

The Long Struggle for Legal Reform

Attempts to legislate against child labor consistently failed. The wording of most state laws left them open to interpretation so they could be evaded by employers, as well as by parents in need of children's wages. Managers often denounced attempts to curb child labor as "abuses of parents' rights." Yet reformers persisted and, by 1912, thirty-eight states had some legal restrictions regarding the employment of children.

The Beveridge Bill

In 1906, Indiana Republican Senator Albert J. Beveridge (1862-1927) proposed a federal child labor bill that would prohibit interstate commerce of products from any businesses that hired children under fourteen. The Senator believed that private industrial interests made state laws ineffective and he urged a national solution to the problem. The NCLC rallied behind the Beveridge Bill, although Theodore Roosevelt did not back it, offering instead a federally-funded study of the child labor problem. The following editorial cites some reasons why the Beveridge Bill went down to defeat.

Source: Editorial, "Child Labor Laws," *New York Times*, January 28, 1907.

Against Senator Beveridge's bill prohibiting transportation in inter-State commerce of products of any factory or mine in which children under fourteen years of age are permitted to work, three objections: (1) The measure, if enacted, will cure but a very small part of the evil at which it is aimed; not more than one-sixth of children below the age of fourteen performing manual labor in the United States are making any contribution whatever to inter-State commerce (2) the bill is a direct encouragement of helpless inefficiency on the part of State Governments which would lead to a large extension of the powers of the Federal Government (3) the bill not only immensely extends the sweep of Federal control over State affairs, but...would reduce powers and functions of State Legislatures to a degree that would leave them no power of regulation save within a diminished area of minor and strictly local matters.

A special bulletin of the Census Bureau shows that in 1900 there were 1,750,178 children between ten and fifteen years of age employed in manual labor. Of this number 1,054,446 are employed in agriculture, and are excepted from the operation of the bill. It is further shown that 138,065 children are engaged in domestic service or as servants or waitresses in restaurants. There remain, therefore, 557,717 children below the age of fourteen who work in mines and factories or are employed as office boys, messengers, bellboys, and in other like callings. Probably not over 300,000 children in the entire country take part in the production of commodities entering into inter-State commerce....It may be said at once that child labor is an evil; it is cruel; it is wasteful of the productive forces of the Republic; it tends to mental and physical degeneration. For our part, we are inclined to insist that it is not worthwhile to make further breaches in the Constitution, and new and large transfers of power to the Federal Government, for the attainment of a result so deplorably imperfect. We must still depend upon State laws to protect one-half of the children who should be protected....

The vital defect and wrong of Senator Beveridge's bill is that it strikes at innocent goods in order to punish the guilty producer....

The Keating-Owen Act

In September of 1916, Congress passed the first federal child labor law, although it applied only to businesses engaged in interstate and foreign commerce. The Keating-Owen Child Labor Act, signed by President Woodrow Wilson, stipulated the following:

• Interstate shipment of any goods produced by children under fourteen years of age or by children fourteen to sixteen who worked more than eight hours a day, prohibited.

• It is illegal to employ children under sixteen years in mines and quarries and children under the age of fourteen in mills, canneries, and factories.

• Children shall be limited to working six days a week

- Children shall not be permitted to work past 7: 00 p.m.
- Factory owners shall be required to verify birth certificates of child employees or face imprisonment.

The business community, particularly managers of Southern textile mills, fought the Keating-Owen Act. Roland Dagenhart of Charlotte, North Carolina, claimed in federal district court that:

> "it deprived his sons of the right to work in the cotton mill where they were currently employed."

On June 3, 1918, the Supreme Court declared the Act "unconstitutional" because it:

> "denied children the freedom to go to work," *and* "violated states' rights....Only individual states had the power to regulate child labor conditions and control business."

Not until 1941 would the Supreme Court finally approve legislation regulating child labor in America.

In 1919, Congress managed to pass a second child labor bill by attaching it to a tax act. This bill to ban child labor placed a ten percent tax on profits of businesses hiring children under fourteen. It also reduced children's working hours and raised the minimum age to fourteen for most occupations and sixteen for night work or work in mines. Documentary proof of age was required. The result was a fifty percent decrease in child labor.

By 1922, this law had also been declared "unconstitutional" by the Supreme Court, who claimed "Congress had "overstepped its authority," ruling it "unlawful to regulate child labor through taxes." The number of working children, as well as the hours they worked, immediately increased.

Constitutional Amendment Proposed and Opposed

Determined child-savers then sought an amendment to the U.S. Constitution that would abolish child labor forever. In 1924, Congress approved an amendment prohibiting child labor, but when it was submitted to the states, only twenty-eight out of thirty-six required would ratify it. The following selection is an example of the strong and emotional opposition to the proposed constitutional amendment.

Source: "Objections to the Child Labor Amendment," *Manufacturers Record*, September 4, 1924. Found in *Annals of America*, 1924, #80, pp. 422-423.

The Child Labor Amendment is not legislation in the interest of children but legislation which would mean the destruction of manhood and womanhood through the destruction of the boys and girls of the country....Massachusetts, which was for so many years noted for its work in behalf of eliminating child workers from factory life, is now aggressively fighting the proposed amendment realizing that it would endanger the very existence of this government....This proposed amendment is fathered by Socialists, Communists, and Bolshevists. They are the active workers in its favor. They look forward to its adoption as giving them the power to nationalize the children of the land and bring about in this country the exact conditions which prevail in Russia....If adopted, this amendment would be the greatest thing ever done in America in behalf of the activities of hell. It would make millions of young people under eighteen years of age idlers in brain and body, and thus make them the devil's best workshop. It would destroy the initiative and self-reliance and manhood and womanhood of all the coming generations....It would be worse than folly for people who realize the danger of this situation to rest content under the belief that this amendment cannot become a part of our Constitution. The only thing that can prevent its adoption will be active, untiring work on the part of every man and woman who appreciates its destructive power and who wants to save the young people of all future generations from moral and physical decay under the domination of the devil himself.

"Stoop Labor"

This little girl, photographed by Hine, worked all day in a cotton field.

In spite of the Fair Labor Standards Act which became law in 1938, agricultural workers are not fully protected. Young people under sixteen can still be found in fields across America, picking vegetables and berries for about fifteen cents a crate. Many leave school to help families at harvest times. Children are exposed to life-threatening chemical pesticides sprayed on crops. Agribusiness employers argue that farm work demands longer hours and that being outdoors is "healthy for kids." Some say children are preferred to pick crops like beans and strawberries since, "Being closer to the ground, kids can reach those plants better." Parents who are migrant workers often depend upon their children's help for survival. Schooling is disrupted and laws difficult to enforce because families are on the move continually, as they follow harvests. The author of the following selection discusses a study of children at "stoop labor" undertaken by the American Friends Service Committee.

Source: *Child Labor in Agriculture*, Summer, 1970. (Philadelphia, PA: AFSC, 1971). Found in Ronald Taylor, *Sweatshops in the Sun: Child Labor on the Farm*, (Boston, MA: Beacon Press, 1973), p. 5.

In 1970, American Friends Service Committee investigators went to Oregon, Washington State, California, Ohio, and Maine and reported one fourth of farm wage workers in the U.S. to be under the age of sixteen, and many, less than six years old. The AFSC estimated that children comprised 75% of the labor force at harvest time.

In the following excerpt, children working in the fields in the early 1970s, reminds the author of "sweatshops" of an earlier era.

Source: Ronald Taylor, *ibid.*, pp. 94-97, 183-184.

Each summer in Oregon, 30,000 to 35,000 children eight to fifteen are bussed from school to work in the strawberry and pole bean fields....The child labor scene is reminiscent of the sweatshop scene of the 1930s...children who work in agriculture are, for the most part, exempted from child labor laws and are practically abandoned to the discretion or whim of whoever's farm they are working on....It should be intolerable for a sizable segment of a major industry to depend upon child labor for its survival. In America in 1970, it is not only tolerated, it is encouraged....

* * * * * * *

Protecting our children — America's future — from exploitation in the workplace is a fundamental duty of the Labor Department.

— Elizabeth H. Dole
former U.S. Secretary of Labor
New York Times, February 5, 1990

Suggestions For Further Reading

Atkin, S. Beth, *Voices From the Fields: Children of Migrant Farm Workers Tell Their Stories*, Boston, NY, Toronto, London: Little, Brown & Co., 1993.

Bequele, Assefa and Jo Boyden, *Combating Child Labour*. Geneva, Switzerland: International Labour Office, 1988.

Cahn, Rhoda & William, *No Time for School, No Time for Play: The Story of Child Labor in America*, NY: Julian Messner, 1972.

Colman, Penny, *Mother Jones and the March of the Mill Children*, CT: Millbrook, 1995. (elementary)

Gutman, Judith, *Lewis Hine and the American Social Conscience*, NY: Walker, 1967.

Freedman, Russell, *Kids at Work: Lewis Hine and the Crusade Against Child Labor*, New York: Clarion Books, 1994.

Hawes, Joseph M., *The Children's Rights Movement: A History of Advocacy and Protection*, Boston: Twayne Publishers/Division of G. K. Hall & Co., 1991.

Knight, William James, *The World's Exploited Children: Growing Up Sadly*, Washington, D. C., U.S. Dept. of Labor, Bureau of Labor Affairs, Monograph #4, March, 1980.

Meltzer, Milton, *Cheap Raw Material: How Our Youngest Workers Are Exploited and Abused*, NY: Viking Press, 1994.

Stein, R. Conrad, *The Story of Child Labor Laws*, Chicago, Illinois: Children's Press, (Cornerstones of Freedom Series), 1984.

Trattner, Walter I., *Crusade for the Children: A History of the National Child Labor Committee and Child Labor Reform in America*, Chicago, IL: Quadrangle, 1970.

Weisman, JoAnne B., ed., *The Lowell Mill Girls: Life in the Factory*. Lowell, MA: Discovery Enterprises, Ltd., 1991.

Recommended Fiction:

Collier, James Lincoln and Christopher Collier, *The Clock*, NY: Delacorte Press, 1992.

McCully, Emily Arnold, *The Bobbin Girl*, NY: Dial Press, 1996. (elementary)

Peck, Robert Newton, *Arly*, NY: Walker and Co., 1989.

Paterson, Katherine, *Lyddie*, NY: Lodestar/Puffin, 1991, 1992.

Stoler, Sigmund, *Working in Darkness - A Play About Coal Mining*, Carlisle, MA: Discovery Enterprises, Ltd., 1996.

Williams, Sherley Anne, *Working Cotton*, New York: Voyager/Harcourt Brace, 1992.

About the Editor

Juliet Haines Mofford holds degrees from Tufts and Boston University. She has taught both elementary and secondary levels in Japan, Spain, and the West Indies. She was a reference librarian before becoming a professional museum educator and community exhibits coordinator in Maine and, later, for the Lowell National Historic Park. A free-lance writer for over twenty-five years, two of her books on New England history received American Association for State & Local History Certificates of Commendation. The mother of three adult children, she lives with her husband in Massachusetts. She currently works as a consultant for Museum Education Services, developing museums-to-schools curricula and Living History dramatic programs for historical societies. Besides a passion for turning young people on to history, her other special interests are travel, multiculturalism, film, women's history and gender issues, and consumer-advocacy.

Ms. Mofford certainly does not believe that kids earning money is a bad thing or that it is necessarily exploitative. She still feels a sense of pride when recalling that at the age of eleven, she became the first girl in Davenport, Iowa, ever hired for an after school newspaper delivery route.

Ms. Mofford also edited *Cry "Witch": The Salem Witchcraft Trials - 1692* and *Talkin' Union: The American Labor Movement* for this *Perspectives on History Series* from Discovery Enterprises, Ltd.